# Outsourcing Essentials for Podcaster

## The Secrets to Hiring On-Demand Talent on a Beach Hut Budget

*by James Martell*

Clearbrook Web Services Inc.
1415 Maple Street
White Rock BC Canada
V4B 5C5

www.podcastingmastery.com
helpdesk@podcastingmastery.com

# DISCLAIMER

This workbook has been written to provide information about developing a successful podcast that will impress all who hear it. Every effort has been taken to make this workbook as complete, helpful and accurate as possible.

This workbook is intended to be educational and instructional. The author and/or the publisher do not guarantee that the information contained in this workbook is comprehensive or complete, and will not be responsible for any errors or omissions. The author and/or publisher bear neither liability nor responsibility to any person or entity with respect to any loss or damage caused or alleged to be caused directly or indirectly by the information in this workbook.

# TABLE OF CONTENTS

## INTRODUCTION

**Imagine having the time and money to follow your passions and live life on your own terms**

Hi, my name is James Martell and I'm the host of the popular *Podcasting Mastery* podcast, broadcast weekly from the **Secret Beach Hut Studio**. I've been podcasting for more than 12 years and over that time I've learned the secrets of how to use outsourcing to create the ultimate, stress-free lifestyle business.

I have created this eBook, *Outsourcing Essentials for Podcasters: The Secret to Hiring On-Demand Talent on a Beach Hut Budget,* to teach you everything you need to know about developing your lifestyle business in a way that allows you to spend less time actually doing business, and more time doing all the things that matter most to you!

I'm going to teach you the strategies you need to know so you can build both a passive monthly income stream and develop passive ways of finding new clients and customers for your business.

As the host of **Podcasting Mastery** podcast, you probably know that I get to interview a lot of very successful podcasters. One of the things I've found they all say over and over again is, that starting their own podcast and managing it was *way* more work than they ever expected!

They also say something like: "I should have hired some help much earlier on in the process, and if I had done of done that, I would have been way further ahead today!"

I also suspect this is a primary reason for the dreaded **"pod-fade"** that many of us have heard of.

Some of you may have even experienced it.

We start our podcast with great intentions, but we underestimate the workload and skill set required. Many podcasters who have had a great opportunity, end up quitting purely because they're completely overloaded and overwhelmed by the process.

**I don't want this to happen to you!**

Rather, imagine waking up in the morning to a message from your **virtual assistant** (VA), who is letting you know:

- Show notes and audio for your latest episode are done
- Episode is now "live" on your website and SEO optimized
- Podcast directories have been updated with the latest edition
- Facebook, Twitter, LinkedIn and YouTube are updated

- Newsletter subscribers have the episode in their inbox

**Sounds amazing, right?**

Well hang on because I'm not finished yet!

They also let you know that they've confirmed your next four guests, and they're preparing your episode outlines for you. I think you would agree as a podcaster, that this would be a **pretty good start to your day!**

It's all possible and I'm going to tell you how you can have a stress-free podcasting business just like mine, through the magic of outsourcing.

## MP3 AUDIO INTERVIEW

Outsourcing Essentials for Podcasters - The Secrets to Hiring Talent on a Beach Hut Budget

Listen here:

http://podcastingmastery.com/outsourcing360/

Password: outsourcing360

# CHAPTER 1:
# MY STORY
# AND OUTSOURCING
# EXPERIENCE

**So what's my story with respect to outsourcing?**

Let me take you back to 2004...

At the time I was running a publishing company up in Vancouver, Canada and we were hiring locals to do much of our work. We needed **writers**, we needed **editors** – we needed a variety of people to build our **online business**.

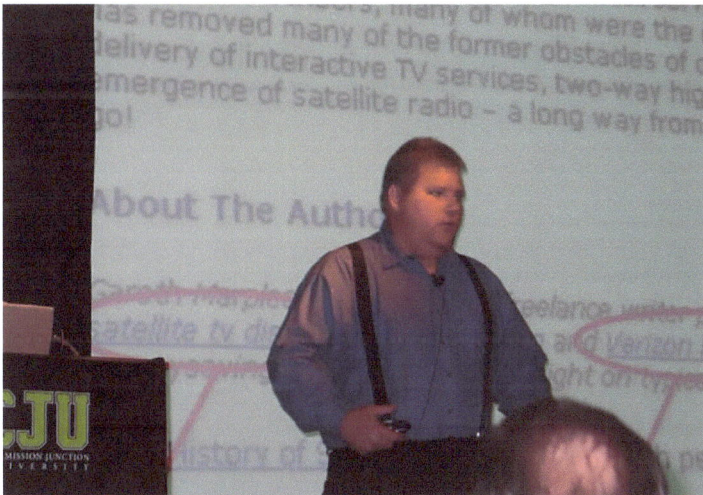

I happened to be invited down to Santa Barbara, California to do a talk at **Commission Junction University,** and part of the talk covered how we went about hiring local people and local talent to assist us with the development of our business.

At the end of that talk, I was approached by one of my students at that time.

**He simply came up to me and said: "I just use Elance."**

I had spent the last 20 minutes going into great detail about how we ran ads in the local newspaper, how we had project descriptions, how we would interview over the phone, and everything we had to do, to do it successfully.

And this student of mine comes up to me and says: "I just use Elance."

I had no idea what they were talking about, so I asked: "What's Elance?"

He explained that it was a website where *thousands* of talented individuals from all over the world were looking for work. All you had to do was post your project, and people would actually bid on the job you needed done. You could then search through the applicants, and hire the best person to do the work for you!

**And I thought, "That's interesting. I'll check that out."**

When I got home, I signed up for a free account at Elance and started posting projects. At the time I had a small office and a few staff members, mainly writers and researchers.

So I started outsourcing projects to others through the Elance system simultaneously and before you knew it, we were not only more productive (because of the interface Elance was providing to us to build our freelance team) but our costs were *dramatically less* than what we were spending locally – upwards of **60-70**% less!

This was possible because these freelancers are located all over the world and I didn't have to treat them as staff, meaning:

- I didn't have to remit payroll
- I didn't have to do the government remittances
- There was no worker's compensation
- I didn't need an office for staff
- And there were great savings in being able to have all of these people work online

I also found out that we had more talent to select from. I was also able to hire them on demand, and they weren't sitting around in the office like our regular staff at the times when work was a little bit slower. I also found the work was *much* higher in quality, because we were dealing with people who were, typically, more professional.

It didn't take long – only about 45 days – before I decided to **shut the office down** and move everything into the Elance system.

And we have never looked back!

That was in 2004. Fast-forward to today.

**It's now 2016.**

I've had the opportunity to build a tremendous online business and I've done it all through outsourcing.

I've outsourced about **1,400 projects** to date, and there's no sign of letting up. It has had a profound impact on my business, and if you're looking to trim back, maybe do a little less work, or maybe increase the quality of the work that you're outputting, I think you'll find the information in this eBook will have a have a **profound** impact on your business too!

Now, I must also say in the recent years **Elance** has rebranded, and has now become a company called **Upwork.** In the next chapter, we're going to talk about how to use **Upwork** to hire low cost, high-quality, on demand talent for your podcast.

## WHY ARE SOME SO RESISTANT TO OUTSOURCING?

**Now before we get talking about Upwork and how to go about hiring low-cost talent, let's talk a little bit about why some are so resistant to outsourcing.**

I know over the years I've run a number of courses on a variety of topics and, without fail, all of those courses always have an outsourcing component. That's because it doesn't matter what you're doing, you can always improve the quality of work being done. You can *always* increase your productivity and output by getting additional people involved.

With this in mind, I've always added an outsourcing component to my courses – no matter what the course is about. And even though I was including it, I was still getting a lot of resistance to outsourcing. So I had to dig in and figure out why.

### Why the resistance?

I found out that many students would say to me, **"I don't know how or where to outsource."**

They also said things like: **"I don't know what to say ...I don't want to waste my money ...I have a fear of looking foolish and not really being up to par on communicating with the freelancer ...and the "I need to learn-to-do-everything-first syndrome."**

Or they have a hard time letting go and letting someone else take care of it for them. Or they just think it's faster if they do it themselves. Or they have what I call the **"Brooke-syndrome"**, which is the same as when I attempted to help my little granddaughter tie her shoes and she looked at me and said: **"I can do it myself!"**

And I thought, "Oh, there's a lesson there."

So again, in this book *Outsourcing Essentials for Podcasters: The Secret to Hiring On-Demand Talent on a Beach Hut Budget* we're going to cover:

- What to say when POSTING a job so you get the *absolute* best price.
- What to look for when HIRING freelancers, so you get the absolute *best-quality* work.
- What to expect to PAY for each job, so you don't pay *too* much.
- What to take into consideration when AWARDING the job, so that your money is *safe* and you get back *exactly* what you want.
- What to do to KEEP the job on track, so you get *what* you want, *when* you want it.
- What to do to WRAP-UP the job, so *everybody* leaves happy.
- How to surround yourself with a VIRTUAL TEAM who *support* you in your podcasting efforts.

And a ton more, including all of my thoughts on hiring your own virtual assistant, and I'm also going to share my very popular **15-minute rule** with you as well.

## HOW DO I GET STARTED?

**I'm going to say the *Number One* challenge most people have is changing their mindset.**

You need to make the decision that you're going to have other people take care of as much work as possible. If you're used to doing things yourself, you're going to have to break that habit. You need to stop the inertia going in the direction of doing everything yourself.

**So you're probably wondering what you should outsource?**

I'll get into more detail in just a moment, but essentially, I recommend almost *everything*. Once you've made the decision that you're not going to do all of this work by yourself, and that you're only going to take care of a few items – I think you'll find outsourcing much easier.

We have a motto around the office here that we've used for years, and I share it with my students and talk about it onstage at events. We also talk about it on the podcast and essentially it is this:

**Do what you do best, outsource the rest.**

If you think about that, it makes sense. If you focus on what you do best and leave the people you have *hired* to do what they do best, you're going to get a much better product (in this case a "podcast") in the end because you're going to have more talent working on your behalf.

**So figure it out like this**:

Instead of learning how to edit your audio or write your SEO-friendly show notes, think about hiring somebody to take care of these items for you. I'm going to discuss this in more detail now, and show you how to build a virtual team of "talents" and "individuals" to support you in your podcasting efforts.

## THE 15-MINUTE RULE

**I have a very interesting story to share.**

Some of it happened not long ago, during one of my courses. One of my students had contacted me beforehand and they were very frustrated. They were having *major* problems with a WordPress technical issue, and they were spending a great deal of time on it.

They had pretty much spent the whole afternoon trying to solve this problem ... and when they still couldn't fix it, they worked into the evening ... and then again the next morning!

By the time they attended the live Q&A and Coaching Session that night, they were incredibly frustrated, so I asked them a very simple question.

**"Have you attempted to hire somebody to solve this problem for you?"**

And they said to me, "No, I hadn't considered it."

I said, "Take **15-minutes** right now; stop everything that you're doing."

"Head over to Upwork, post a project, explain the problem, and then wait for the bids to come in. Award it to the first person you think is suitable to tackle this for you, and then let me know how it goes."

They did that that evening, and the next morning I received an email from them. They were very excited that the problem had been solved. So I asked them: "How much did it cost you to have it fixed?"

**Their answer was, "12 dollars!"**

I can promise you this has completely changed the way they do business online. They no longer struggle with problems. In fact, they now outsource *everything* they do because when they "did the math", they realized they needed to dramatically change their approach when it came to getting things done.

They realized they were attempting to solve a problem themselves that, quite frankly, they weren't qualified to solve. They had spent approximately 12 hours on the problem, and then ended up hiring somebody for **$12** to solve it for them!

Even if they had managed to fix the problem themselves, it would have taken them *12 hours* of their precious time ... so essentially they were working for **$1 per hour!**

Having someone else take care of it for them would have **ONLY COST $12!**

Luckily, they realized that working for $1 per hour *wasn't* going to get them where they wanted to go.

**So the 15-minute rule goes like this.**

If anything I happen to be working on in my business (and I do mean anything) has me struggling for more than 15-minutes, I stop immediately.

I then head over to Upwork, and spend the next 15 minutes detailing what the problem is, and then post it as a job. Before long I find some help; someone to take care of it for me so I don't end up just like that student, wasting hours and hours and hours of time, trying to solve a problem I'm not technically educated to handle.

**This is the primary mistake so many of us make – we attempt to do the work of others!**

For example. Maybe you're not qualified to write SEO-friendly notes. Can you learn how to do it? Sure, but why do that when you can find an individual who can do it for you at a very low cost? Why do it yourself?

If you're going through my podcasting training, you will notice that I'm laying all the groundwork for all of this, which is essentially to assist you in building a podcast that does the work for you, so you don't have to.

In the training, I talk about **Strategically Developing Episodes** on topics of great interest to your ideal clients. And then scattering those episodes all over the Internet within the podcasting directories, social media, and Google, to attract, warm up, and demonstrate your expertise, and then direct those ideal clients back to you.

Essentially, the beautiful thing about a podcast is that you can do exactly that. You can scatter your episodes all over the Internet, use them to attract your ideal client, warm them up, demonstrate your expertise, and direct them back to your website or back to you, so you can do business with them.

The objective in creating a podcast is not to increase your workload. On the contrary, your podcast should dramatically *reduce* your workload.

# CHAPTER 2:
# WHICH JOBS SHOULD A
# PODCASTER OUTSOURCE?

It's a great question and I feel that you, as the host of your own show, should be behind the microphone. Other than that, everything else for the most part should be taken care of for you by your virtual team.

## WRITING

I would suggest hiring a **writer** to develop all of your text for your show.

If you're just starting, you're going to find as you go through the process of setting up your podcast, there are all types of texts needed. Your show descriptions, your personal bio ... there are just a number of things that need to be written.

I would suggest hiring a writer to develop *all* of your texts. In addition of course, once your podcast is up and running, each episode is going to require some high-quality, search engine-optimized show notes that you can include, along with the audio to promote your episode.

## GRAPHIC DESIGN

I suggest you also hire a **graphic designer** to develop all of the graphics for your podcast.

One of the interesting things about podcasting is, it gives us the ability to distribute these episodes far and wide. And that's great, but it would be really nice if we had graphics that would actually promote each episode, and having a graphic designer at your fingertips to do so, is a great way to go about it.

You also find if you're in the setup process, and you're setting up graphics for Spreaker, iTunes, various podcasting directories, your social media, your own website, etc., that you're going to need different sized graphics in many cases.

A graphic designer can help you with that quite easily. You should also keep in mind that there's nothing *worse* than homemade graphics. **They stand out like a sore thumb, so don't fall into that trap!**

## VOICE WORK

I suggest hiring some **voice talent**; somebody to help you voice your intro and your outro.

If you're going to play radio-style ads in the middle of your show, they can definitely help you with that. It's also worth hiring a few different people so you can mix it up a bit.

## AUDIO EDITING

I suggest hiring an **editor** to handle the audio for each of your episodes. Let them remove the "um's and ah's". And let them add the intro, the outro, and the radio-style ads.

## SUPPORT

And *most* importantly, hire yourself a **virtual assistant** to assist you in all layers of your podcast.

# CHAPTER 3:
# WHAT DO I SAY
# WHEN POSTING A JOB?

This is one of the questions I receive a lot and it's a good question because one of the roles of a job description is to clearly detail exactly what you want to have done – or at least it *should!*

And if it doesn't, that's where problems begin. It's *so* important when posting a job that you know, and can articulate, the details of **exactly** what you want to be done.

Let me give you an example: I'll pull one right out of one of our internal manuals here.

Let's say you're looking to have the graphics created for your podcast and you want to post the project on Upwork, to find a graphic designer to take care of this for you.

The first thing you would do, of course, is login to Upwork and then click on **Post Job.** You would then select the category for the project. And in this case, it would be **Design and Creative**, and the sub-category would be **Graphic Design**.

You would then *describe* the job by giving it a name.

For example: **"Graphic Designer: Podcast Artwork/Thumbnails/Social Media Cover Art."**

Then you would describe the work to be done.

## JOB DESCRIPTION SAMPLE

Let me pull up one of our internal manuals here, to give you an idea of how I would write a job description.

**It would be something similar to:**

*Hi, it's James Martell here. Thank you for bidding on my project.*

*I'm looking to have 9-10 graphics created that includes the artwork for the podcast directories, 2 thumbnail images in various sizes, and the social media cover art for Facebook, Twitter, and LinkedIn.*

*I would like to look and feel for the images to match the look and feel of our website on the link below.*

*I would like all the images to be the same over all to keep it simple and to keep the branding throughout the websites.*

*I would like you to create the look at feel of the graphics first and once we sign off on the look and feel, you can then use it to design the other images.*

*Once the project is complete, I would like the raw data files as a .psd.*

*And I would like the thumbnail images to be provided to me with both a white background and a transparent background.*

*Thank you so much for bidding on my project. I look forward to seeing your bid.*

*Thank you,*

*James.*

*PS. I will include the text, my headshot, and another image for the job once it has been awarded.*

And of course, if you are a student of my **Podcasting Mastery Course**, you have in your possession a copy of my workbook **Hiring Great Freelancers: Grow your Podcast Faster with On-Demand Talent,** which includes all of the pre-written project descriptions and work orders I use internally for hiring writers, graphic designers, voice talents, audio editor, producers, and virtual assistants.

# CHAPTER 4:
# WHAT DO I NEED TO LOOK AT
# WHEN HIRING A FREELANCER?

Now that you've posted the job, you will notice quickly that talent from all over the planet will bid on your project. You can usually tell that these are good people. They are typically hard workers, proficient in their areas of expertise, and are trustworthy.

**I've hired literally hundreds and hundreds of freelancers over the years!**

They're great people – I enjoy working with them, and I think you will as well. With this in mind though, when you award a project to someone new, it's important to check them out first.

You do that by looking at their feedback, checking out their ratings, and taking note of how many hours they've worked for others. In other words, you **"dig"** through their portfolio.

Upwork gives you the tools to check out a freelancer that you are considering hiring, so you can have a good look at what they've done for others. Take some time to *really* read the feedback, review their ratings, and dig through their portfolio.

**A little tip here:** one of the tools within the Upwork system that you can utilize is the field that shows you how many hours they've worked. This is important to look at because if someone has a 100% feedback rating, but has only worked one hour, you should probably move on. Whereas, if somebody has a 90% feedback rating, and they have a thousand hours under their belt, you'd be better off to go with the talent that has a thousand hours, versus the talent that has one!

Use your common sense when you're in there. It's pretty straight-forward and I think you'll find that you'll get comfortable there very quickly.

**Another quick tip is to check out where they live.**

I will say without fail, I never hire writers from countries where English is not the native speaking language unless, I'm *completely* confident it's an **American** or **Canadian** living overseas. Even though freelancers in those countries are very good (and are often very persuasive when it comes to convincing you to let them take on your writing projects), I would *highly* recommend that you don't use them. They just don't understand the nuances of our language, and there'll be far too much editing on the back end.

I do find, however, people from those countries are great at **programming**, great at **graphic design**, and more of the **hands-on stuff**. Just stay away from anything to do with writing with respect to your projects.

# CHAPTER 5:
# WHAT DO I NEED TO BUDGET
# FOR EACH JOB?

**Now as far as the budget goes, you want to know what each job will cost, right?**

It's a good question, and if you've ever hired someone locally in North America, Europe or Australia, you'll find that the prices I'm about to share with you are fraction of what you would normally pay. I mentioned this earlier – how I have hired local people in the past but found I could *cut my costs by 60-70%* by hiring people online to do the same work.

That was through the Elance system at the time (now Upwork), and it still rings true today. So let me share a few numbers with you to give you a general idea what you should expect to pay when you use the Upwork system to hire for these types of jobs.

To have an **Intro and Outro** for your podcast professionally produced by a Voice Talent who will not only read for you and provide the professional voicing, but who will also add your music and the sound effects that you need to give you a full production – I typically pay **$35-$50** in the Upwork system.

To have the **show's artwork** created, I typically pay between **$30** and **$50**. If I include a lot of other artwork with it such as a logo, social media, artwork as we talk about in the example earlier—then you may be heading towards **$100** for all of your graphics.

Those are typically the types of prices you'll expect to pay during the setup phase of your podcast.

Now ongoing — when you are recording your ongoing episodes, you will need some **audio editing** and I typically pay between **$15** and **$25** per episode, depending on its length. It could be a 30-minute episode, or it could be 60-minute one.

You also need to have some professionally written **show notes** created, and you can see a good example of these at www.podcastingmastery.com.

Just take a look at any of the episodes. I get a lot of feedback on how good the show notes are, and I have a great writer that I found on Upwork who writes all of my show notes for this podcast, and others that my company manages for clients. For show notes I typically pay somewhere between **$15 and $20** per episode.

And then there's your **personal virtual assistant** that you can hire on-demand for typically **$5 to $7** per hour, and I can pretty much guarantee you will quickly wonder how you ever lived without them.

I'll talk more about hiring an *amazing* virtual assistant (VA) in an upcoming chapter.

# CHAPTER 6:
# WHAT DO I NEED TO CONSIDER
# WHEN AWARDING A PROJECT?

**Another great question!**

You've gone ahead and posted the job, the freelancers have come in and they've bid on it from all over the world. You have a general idea of what to look for because of what we have discussed earlier, and you know roughly what you can expect to pay to have the work completed.

You've also looked at their **feedback**, you've looked at their **ratings**, you've looked at their **portfolio**, and now you're ready to award them the job.

What else, though, do you need to consider when actually awarding the job?

## HOW TO SET MILESTONES

This is where Upwork comes to the rescue and provides you with some tools within its system that I highly recommend you consider using. The first one is their **"Milestone"** feature.

Milestones give you the ability to chop the job up into pieces. If it's just a little job, like having your episode outline edited, one milestone will suffice. If it's for your show notes, same thing – one milestone is more than enough.

However, if it's an ongoing project or a larger project, then you can chop it up into smaller milestones and you can pay as you go. So, instead of having to fund a large project all upfront, you can fund it in increments.

This will help you with your budgeting, and also keep your money *safe*.

## HOW TO USE THE
## ESCROW FEATURE

The second feature within the Upwork system that I highly recommend you consider using is their **"Escrow System"**.

Once you've setup a milestone, you are then prompted to fund it, and you will need to do this. Now, the beautiful thing about the escrow system within Upwork is, you do not release the money to the freelancer until *you have received the work and you're happy with it!*

So definitely use milestones, and definitely use escrow system.

# CHAPTER 7:
# WHAT DO I NEED TO DO TO KEEP THE JOB ON TRACK?

**This is another question that's really worth thinking about.**

Within the Upwork system, if you're dealing with a freelancer, and you let them slide on their deadlines (let's say you've setup a milestone to be completed by next Wednesday, and by the end of the day you have not alerted them that they are missing their deadline) you are *essentially agreeing* that it's okay.

Whereas, if you alert them that *they are about to miss the deadline* – and it is not acceptable – then you've got some grounds to work with, and you don't typically have to say anything more.

It usually lights are fire under their butt a little bit, so to speak, and gets them rolling. But don't let it slide from there. If you've got a project that is a week-long or 10-days long, don't wait until the *last minute* to find out that they're behind ... or they're sick ... or they've gone on holidays ... or they've dropped the ball somehow.

## IT'S IMPORTANT TO STAY IN TOUCH

Another great **safeguard** when you award a project is to stay in touch with the freelancer through the messaging system within Upwork. Let them know that you'd like to see a first draft on the first day.

This is a game where a milestone can come in. Don't let it *slide* for a long period of time and have no communication, especially on longer jobs. **You want to stay on top of them**. And if you keep the lines of communication open, you'll find it will really help you to keep the job on track.

# CHAPTER 8:
# HOW DO I WRAP UP THE JOB?

**Everything is going great.**

You've got the project back and you're very happy with it. You're ready to sign off on the completed work and release the escrow. First thing I would do is just double check everything. Make sure that you have *everything*.

If you have graphics done, and graphics created for your podcast, make sure you have all the raw data source files. You need these because if you want to get the graphics modified in the future, you actually have the raw source files that you can then hand to another graphic designer who can *easily* make those changes for you. If you don't have them, you're going to find yourself having to hire a graphic designer to attempt to reproduce them from scratch.

**That's going to cost you a lot more money!**

Whereas, if you just make sure that you have the original source files from the project, then you're going to be fine.

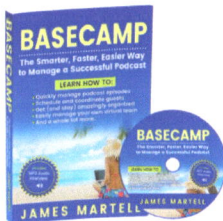

I also recommend putting them somewhere *safe*. I can't tell you how many times I've heard the story that I had them but I can't find them ... or I don't know where I put them ... or they're lost! So I highly recommend taking the time to put them somewhere safe.

Preferably in the Cloud or in **Basecamp**.

Now if you haven't heard of **Basecamp**, it's an **Online Project Management System** that I highly recommend and use personally, and I couldn't begin to fathom having to live without it. I have talked about this amazing online management system extensively in an episode of my *Podcasting Mastery* podcast entitled *Basecamp: The Smarter, Faster, Easier Way to Manage a Successful Podcast.*

If you haven't had a chance to listen to that yet, I recommend that you do so.

You'll find that outsourcing is a powerful tool, combined with an **Online Project Management System** to manage the entire process. With **Basecamp**, I guarantee you'll have a system in place that will help you to dramatically avoid *Pod-fade*, because everything will be so organized and you will be so well taken care of by your team, working in an environment called Basecamp, that you'll wonder how you have ever lived without it as well.

> *Tip: When dealing with freelancers, I also ask them to name their files in a way that makes sense.*
>
> *For example, if they're going to send me the show's artwork, let them label it "show artwork for [whatever your podcast name is]." There's nothing worse than getting a whole bunch of files back from a freelancer that says, "file-01", "file-02", "file-03". I have no idea*

*what those files are, so I ask them to please label them **logically** so they make sense, and so I can tell at a glance what they are. That helps **tremendously** in the organization of your podcast.*

**A few other things to further wrap up the project.**

Ask them to leave feedback on what it was like to work with you as a client. I will usually say something to them to the effect that: "I have just left you a **5-star** rating and some great feedback, would you mind doing something similar for me?" Then I simply end the contract by using a button in the Upwork system designed to do this. **And that's it, you're done!**

## CHAPTER 9:
## WHAT PODCASTERS OUGHT TO KNOW ABOUT HIRING A VIRTUAL ASSISTANT ...AND HOW TO GET IT RIGHT THE FIRST TIME!

I've been alluding to this topic all the way through this eBook, and this essentially came to me after overhearing a podcaster saying to another podcaster: **"Hey! I hired a bunch of VAs."**

And I thought, after listening to a little more of their conversation, that what they had really done was outsource to a variety of freelancers. They had a graphic designer in their camp, they had an audio editor, a writer, and a few others ...and they were *mislabeling* them all **virtual assistants!**

And I thought *"that's very interesting"* because I think before hiring a VA, we should really understand the role of a VA. I've had the opportunity to have a VA work for me for years, and sometimes **two or three** of them – depending on how busy I am.

And it has really helped me to have a life.

Over the years I've had students say to me: "James, I have no idea how you and Arlene get so much done."

They know we do a lot of traveling, lots of trips to **Las Vegas, Disneyland,** and **Disney World** with the **kids** ...and **cruises** ...and **Maui** ...I could go on and on. And they were under the impression that we were doing all of

the work ourselves, when in reality, we are just overseeing the work being done by our freelancers and, more importantly, our virtual assistants.

Your virtual assistant, in my opinion, is not your writer ...or your graphic designer ...or your audio editor ...or your producer ...or any other of
those roles that we've talked about.

Your virtual assistant is just exactly that – they are your **Personal Virtual
Assistant**, and they should be managing your writer, your graphic designer, your audio editor, your producer, and anybody else that you hire.

And all these people should be reporting to your VA, not you!

**But here's the real epiphany: your virtual assistant should also be man-
aging (get ready for it) ...YOU!**

They should be managing your podcasting schedule. They should be
reaching out to potential guests. They should be the one who sends in-
vites to identified targets and asks them to join you on the show.

If you have a virtual producer who's recording your show, they should be
reporting directly to your virtual assistant. Your virtual assistant will coordinate with your audio editor, and your writer, to make sure the show
notes are written properly.

They'll coordinate with the audio editor to make sure that the audio is
properly edited. They will be the one adding the actual episode to your
website, along with the show notes that were written by your writer.
And your virtual assistant will take care of the promotion of each of your
episodes. If you think about what I mentioned earlier; that you could hire
a top quality, brilliant virtual assistant for **$5** to **$7** per hour, why in the
world would you *ever* be doing *any* of this yourself?

**Your VA, in my opinion, should be in charge of your podcast.**

You are the one that shows up each week with the content, you are the one that interviews the guests, and you are the talent. Your VA is your assistant, but they are in charge of your show. It is their responsibility to make sure that the show is organized, recorded, produced, and promoted.

It is their job to make sure everything runs smoothly.

**Now, is it difficult to setup?**

Yes, it is. But this is where my *Podcasting Mastery Course* really shines because it includes all of my step-by-step procedures (as well as all of my internal collateral) to build, setup, and manage a successful podcast.

Let me give you an example, because in addition to more than 300-pages of information you won't get anywhere else, my *Podcasting Mastery Training Manual and Video Series* (where I teach the **8-steps for Creating a Profitable Podcast** – one that not only you will be proud of, but one that will impress all who hear it) all my students also receive:

- All of our internal collateral, including Fill-in-the-Blank templates and worksheets
- Our project descriptions
- Our Work orders
- And all of our Step-by-step procedures so you can do *all* of the work yourself, or better yet, you can hand it off to your personal VA to do the work for you!

This is the *same* collateral I give to my own personal VA, and the same collateral my **VA** gives to our **graphic designer**, our **writer**, our **audio**

**editor,** and our **producer.** And it's all packaged within 4 *extremely com-prehensive* and *attractive* workbooks! You can use the workbooks to do the work yourself, or you could have your VA oversee the work for you.

**It's your choice!**

Now, to find out more about ***Podcasting Mastery: The 8-Steps You Must Follow to Succeed as a Podcaster,*** visit www.podcastingmastery.com/course/

So there you have it ...***Outsourcing Essentials for Podcasters: The Secret to Hiring On-Demand Talent on a Beach Hut Budget.*** I just want to say thanks for reading this eBook and I hope you found it helpful.

Email: helpdesk@podcastingmastery.com
Telephone: (604) 542-0747

Website: www.podcastingmastery.com
Course: www.podcastingmastery.com/course/